SOME DAY

this pain will be useful to you

By **CYRUS AARON**

This book is dedicated to

Derrick "Joe" Edwards

(11.17.1984 – 10.19.2009)

and the many restless souls

in and out of time.

ACKNOWLEDGMENTS

I thank my mother, **Barbara P. McNeal**, for telling me to speak up my entire life. Without you I have no words. Thank you **Granddaddy & Grammy** for being the only constant; you will always be home. To **Dale**, **Dex**, and **Erik**—the OG storytellers. Thank you **Pac** (1971–1996) for making sense of this pain for a little boy on the South Side of Chicago. And to **Kendrick** and **Cole** for picking up where Pac left off. Thanks to **Dr. Pero Dagbovie, Dr. Eric Thomas, Dr. Lee June, Dr. Aime J. Ellis** (1969–2009), **Dr. Richard Thomas, Murray Edwards** and **Anne Graves** for taking me in and giving me direction. To **Leah** for telling me I'm not doing enough with my writing. Thank you for listening and saving all my notes. To **Will, Lindsie, Alex,** and **Lauren** for being there every step of the way. To **Q** for confirming the urgency. A final thanks to my editor, **Ditte Woodson**, and my designer, **Helen Koh**, for embracing my voice and vision.

I'm overwhelmed. I can't dry these tears. Enough with the tears. Everything's a mess. I'm a mess. A flood of emotions. I'm drowning. My sorrow. I'm sorry. Scared of today. Scared for tomorrow. Sleep don't come easy. I weep so easily. I want them to need me. I've gotten soft. The pain don't rub off. These smudged thoughts. All this Black. All this blue. Running ink. Running. All this blood. Another body. His body. Her body. I'm sorry. Too many memorials at once. Death comes in twos. First they took Alton. Then Philando. Took Terrence. Took Keith too. Too many hashtags. Imagine the caskets. Don't imagine the caskets. I know him in that casket. Wasn't no accident. I'm sorry. These tears. I couldn't help him. I can't help it. I see myself. I've seen myself. I've been here before. I've stood here once before. Told myself. I wasn't gon' come here no more. Damn Joe. They brought me back here. You still here. You ain't going nowhere. They stopped you right there. Laid you there. You laid there. I couldn't watch them lay you somewhere. Once again they gon' lay me somewhere. They gon' bring me back. To die here. I'm scared of dying here. I'm dying here. I can't watch another die here. I'm not brave.

If you are silent about your pain, they'll kill you and say you enjoyed it.

— Zora Neale Hurston

There is no greater magnifier to reveal the divide in America's bed than the brutality on Black bodies. Violence against the Negro has a stark way of pulling the covers back, revealing the deep injustice that pushes our moralities to opposite corners. The hole in America's bed sinks deep, a tree trunk of history saddled with supremacy and oppression. For too long we have focused our attention on the depth of the rabbit hole, overlooking the width of hate and how far discrimination stretches the Earth.

The oppressed are always expected to work with so little, even humanity can be rationed in disproportionate shares. The Negro must settle on the wrong side everyday of his life, and find solace in his position. He is given nothing to cover himself, nothing but the thickness of his own skin, while his bedmate is coddled in the cotton-threaded sheets delicately woven by slave hands. He has no assurances to rest his head upon, only hope—the darkest form of control. The Negro must perfect the humility in his gratitude, over spiritualize his lack and conjure up pride from the ashes of his history. He must essentially lie to himself to forget his total well being. He must turn his back on being whole, learn to without certain inalienable rights, forsake his own comfort so that white pride can be at ease in its American ideals and dreams.

With such small space to function, the narcissism of the white imagination is a danger to the Negro, as it has no boundaries. Conceit stirs reckless behavior, but the Negro withdraws, curled into a corner for preservation. His survival is contingent on going unnoticed, by appearing non-threatening and useful. The daily prayer upon lying down is to ask God, what part of himself must he surrender? This prayer is repeated faithfully until he learns what side of his conscious is bearable to sleep on, what is easiest to tolerate in order to rest like his bedmate.

Then he hears the gunshot in the middle of the night, haunted by tragedies his entire existence, the rusty jagged nail sliding down his sensitive conscious. The Negro is easily rattled, while the white imagination snores, even overwhelming the sound of terror. Uncomfortable from every angle the Negro turns to face his white peer to wake him, maybe even to sit up and discuss the constant nightmares. But the white conscious is fast asleep and unmoved, lying with his back to the Negro, and the widespread shame that consumes everything between them.

SOME DAY

this   pain   will   be   useful   to   you

SHORT ESSAYS & POEMS

Marshawn McCarrel took his own life at the young age of 23. He was Leatha's son, a writer, and a Black boy who spoke up for Black lives. I didn't know him, but I am familiar with the burden that finally became much too much for him to bear. From the time we are born we are treated like second class citizens. Society promotes this idea that we are unqualified to freely access all human and civil rights. Being fully human and citizen are truths we shouldn't have to defend, and yet we must, and this is where the conundrum of Black life gets heavy.

America prides herself on a legacy of liberation but has stubbornly refused to share her liberties with all of her children. Marshawn's suicide is the price of speaking triumph in the face of trouble. The fatal agony of pleading for what is rightfully yours. He grew tired, exhausted of being made a fool for having hope in his country. In his attempt to drive out darkness with light, the darkness drove him off the edge of his sanity.

This suffering has existed long before I came into the world. I expect it will continue long after I am gone. Even our cultural champions like, Dr. Martin Luther King Jr. have buckled under the weight of "Blackness." A few years after his beloved "I Have a Dream" speech, Dr. King talked about the dream turning into a nightmare. He said, "some of the old optimism was a little superficial and now it must be tempered with a solid realism."

I didn't expect the man who stood at the mountaintop of hope and optimism to utter such grim words. How could the dream that we all love and commemorate turn into a nightmare for its author? Then again, he was assassinated. All that hope, all that non-violence, 'sweet and docile negro' the media loves to promote, and they shot and killed him. There is nothing sweet and docile about a man being shot in his head by a gunman hiding somewhere in the distance. The reality that it can be any of us, for any given reason, at any given time is the bitter fruit we are tired of being fed.

To be a Black man in this world is to have our sanity, our safety, pulled apart daily by the height of our hopes and by the depth of our circumstances. No matter who we are, or how far we think we've come, we are not insulated from the longstanding threats in a society built on oppression and hate. If heavy is the head that wears the crown, then how heavy is the head hanging at the hand of the crown?

It takes a certain strength and boldness to be Black and a leader of the community.

I am sensitive to the sacrifices required to encourage people to look beyond their circumstances. It's a daunting task to share inner truth when surrounded by external lies. We have to respect and not shun those who choose consciousness and stand on the front lines to challenge the systems so many tolerate.

Marshawn's optimism was admirable. He chose to lead, to march to the end of the tunnel, and it was the light that cost him his life. Days before his suicide he was being recognized for his commitment to the cause—if being affirmed by your people ain't enough to keep going, damn the weight of it all. If walking the red carpet with your mama, and seeing her beam with pride ain't enough, then damn the weight of it all! If love and respect can't encourage us to breathe a little while longer, how much trouble are we in?

Marshawn's demons, the voices in his head exposed a secret—the secret that we have tried to hide in order to appear strong and adequate. Black people are hurting, been hurting for some time now, and for a lot of us suffering is all we know. Sure, we're resilient, but that doesn't make all of this pain and confusion worth it.

Our ability to withstand and overcome does not warrant abuse. It does not mean that it is befitting of us to handle all that we can. I have often felt hope pressuring me from one side, and despair from the other. The weight of both crushing every breath of air these lungs reach for. I'm scared of the day I don't find the strength. I'm not even on the front lines, and I can't recall a time in my life when the walls weren't closing in.

When the first African was stripped of his humanity and forced into slavery, the lie began. The wickedness and greed of the western world decided their road to prosperity and power would be paved on the backs of Africans. And this would be our legacy. Cattle. Expendable subjects—they looked us in our human eyes, and refused to see us as people. The reckless and cruel use of power would not only become a societal standard but common law. We had to accept this lie and take what was given to us. And this is the legacy America bestowed upon us.

Some days I feel like I'm just a number; a body to be counted, and it makes my soul ache. I wish I didn't feel this way, but I've inherited this pessimism. It's the 21st century and massa's voice still echos in the wind. I still hear the chains rustling in the field, the barking hounds close on my trail. Here I am, well-traveled, a playwright, an author, chasing the American Dream, yet I still feel powerless. I still feel vulnerable to the lie, this tainted legacy that can change the course of my life at its discretion.

Legacy is simply a continuous investment to establish a standard, a certain expectation. Very often there is a report issued that confirms our legacy: High probability of imprisonment, high dropout rates, high unemployment rates, etc. We are constantly fed statistics of longstanding inadequacies that essentially penalize us in our everyday lives. A disproportionate number of Black men and women are physically shackled, imprisoned not so much for committing a crime, as for being expected to do so.

I "made it out." I'm one of the lucky few; at least that's what they tell me. But how often are we reminded that you never make it out? The lie is still in control and can pull us back with a simple "Show me your ID." Former tennis star James Blake only had to stand outside of his hotel. Harvard Professor Henry Louis Gates was met by the lie on his front porch. "Show me your freedom papers;" the chains do not fall far from the family tree.

It's always ironic that athletes are the primary examples used to demonstrate the progress of Black America. I'm supposed to listen to an argument about a physical specimen with "freakish" abilities who is a prop to capitalism and corporate agenda, but this superstar figure is likely to be criticized and fined for speaking about the issues concerning his community. Proof that our value is merely dictated by our physical prowess. They want us to just "shut up and play," and that's progress. What could we possibly have to complain about?

Oppression creates greater depths of disproportion with every new generation. It's to the point now that we don't know if the problem is with the individual's choices or the system that perpetuates the range of choices in the first place. That's why mentorship cannot be overlooked; exposure is the key to unlock the dark rooms of circumstance. I've accepted the difficult task of mentoring and working with young men of color. It's rewarding work, but I am reminded of who receives the brunt of this country's atrocities.

You should see my face every time one of our future leaders tells me he wants to play ball, but he's not even on a team. He's aware of the odds, but he'll say anything if it means he doesn't have to struggle anymore. The hoop dream is one of the few examples he's seen produce favorable outcomes of escape. Everywhere these kids look, someone is dressing up disparity and inequality with materialistic nonsense that isn't made for them to begin with.

I want to curse the apparatus producing deferred dreams. It's disgusting to witness the maturation of this lie. We have been exposed to particular tracks, predisposed to a pattern that profits from our obedience. The power players glamorize the feat of the winners, but never give attention to the masses who are sacrificed in the shadows. The frills of a few and the fuss of a bright future is enough for all of us to fall in line. We tighten our own shackles now, just to ensure we have no plans of rocking the boat. And this is all done in the name of tradition. All to keep the lie alive.

I learned how to code switch at the age of seven. My mother transferred me to a new school at the instruction of my teacher. She felt I'd be better off somewhere else. The next thing I know, I'm wearing a uniform, attending Mass, and taking communion. Imagine my shock going from all Black everything to being the token. There's a point in life when every Black person realizes they are Black, and that moment came to me in second grade.

The academic challenge was easy, but the social challenge was the real test. The humor was different; the nuances and word choices were not my own. I had never been the outsider before in reality, but luckily television and Hollywood oddly prepared me for this new terrain. I was used to watching white children interact without me, but now I was expected to participate and live among them. I had to learn how to adapt to a new surrounding, a new tongue, a new layer of skin for survival.

Code switching isn't an easy adjustment, but we learn how to maneuver over time. We should be given credit for our linguistic acrobatics, however, it's never enough. Societal ills disguise so well inside of rules, codes of conduct and progress reports. I was always getting in trouble; I don't remember a report card that didn't flag my behavior. The school's objective was to grow me into their system, instead of helping me grow into myself. Their intent was to teach this Black boy to be proper and meek.

It was weird because they'd recognize my intelligence, but would not hesitate to undermine my humanity. My culture. My "Blackness." This is my issue with most of America's institutions; their methods don't incorporate us for who we are, but for what they want out of us. The picture always paints the same. The white savior will redeem and civilize the uncouth Negro. As if, we can't help ourselves. As if our distress isn't tied to the scarcity of resources: the lack of proper housing practices, the lack of adequately funded schools, or the lack of local government intervention that doesn't equate to more policing. Institutional racism is the hand holding our communities down while pushing the residents to give up on their neighborhoods, and seek refuge in predominantly white spaces.

Everyday I left my friends for opportunity, for something better. I left the people who understood me for a world that barely accepted me. The system is built to make us believe we have no other option. If we want what's best, we must leave our own. And that's what I did. That was the decision my mother thought she had to make. A decision she was encouraged to make. It wasn't her fault, nor was it my teachers for wanting better, but we have to challenge the systemic racism that would make this decision necessary for a parent and their seven-year-old. I was in the second grade when I learned about the miseducation of the Negro. Lucky me.

STRANGE FRUIT

Color encourages order

and mama works   too hard
for him to   play hard
and dirty up that
nice school   uniform.

He has five days to stretch it to
                        Friday.

The main objective somewhere between
making   high marks

and making   perfect
                        attendance,
is to make it through the week;

he can't afford to make mistakes.

                But no matter how much
his mother   tries
she can't   iron out
the urban in his   creases,

can't hold back enough bleach
to dim the contrast
between his   neck
and   collar.

Single parent home
work does not give her the time

to watch him enough
to wash out

the neighborhood in his speech
without washing him out his culture,
momma just want her boy to be
                        cultured,

but not at the risk of who he is.

In moments of reflection, I wonder about his final words. I think about what Tamir Rice could've possibly said to himself before he was murdered. I wonder what silly thought made him laugh before the world fell on top of that smile. As an only child, I had countless isolated moments tearing up the neighborhood with me, myself, and I. My imagination allowed me to be anything I wanted to be. I just hope on that horrific day in the park, he was the good guy saving the world. I hope he spent his final minutes being every bit of child a 12-year-old can be.

There's an old gospel song that says tragedies are commonplace. We don't reckon how common, until it knocks on our front door. Some messengers are familiar but at a safe distance: a wailing ambulance barreling through the neighborhood going somewhere else, or a bold headline in the morning paper about someone else. Distance is a luxury, a convenient space for self-preservation. But this wealth of distance isn't afforded to us.

We are familial people—kindred. I am convinced that we are the only people who when something happens to one of us, it happens to all of us. We celebrate the good, feel the bad, and reflect on the in between.

Despite the legacy of systems and industries fixed on breaking us apart, we are still deeply rooted. *We all we got.*

The digital age of access confirms this invisible thread. Social media has not only increased the rate in which we connect, but has confirmed why we must stay connected as a culture. We are not surprised at all by the evidence that race issues still exist in America; we are more so disheartened by the frequency of that proof. I am beyond tired of waking up to the news of another Black man, woman, or child being murdered.

I don't know much about Cleveland. I don't know what the neighborhoods are like or how the houses look, but when Tamir Rice was murdered, tragedy knocked on my front door as if it too were my home. Before the onslaught of headlines and alerts I was in a good mood, and then my smile felt shameful. What could I possibly be so happy about? How dare I marry joy with my "Blackness?"

It's this moment that every brother and sister I know has experienced, and reliving this moment over and over again is why we hold onto so much anger. What do you do when your country is your agitator? How do you live in a society that has a history of turning its back on you? Of pulling its weapon on you? America has taken everything: our blood, our humanity, our souls, and it often reminds us how quickly it can get under our skin. We are being trapped and cornered, and no one is listening to us, but us. Tamir never had a chance; a target from the day he was born, and when the bully showed up he was alone. We'll never know the last thing that made him laugh. I just hope he laughed.

Back in college, I had the great opportunity to study abroad—thank you to Dr. Folu Ogundimu and Dr. Connie Currier at Michigan State University for providing such a life changing experience. I spent six weeks in Ghana, West Africa and for the first time in my life I was in a world where Black was infinite, and I loved it! What I didn't love, however, was the moment someone yelled at me "Hey Nigga!"

It was so misplaced I thought *maybe the heat is getting to me. Who in this beautiful far away land of brown people would call me a nigga?* It didn't make any sense, and then it happened again, "Hey Nigga!" I was used to hearing it but not here, not on this sacred ground. I turned around and B-lined right to the group of teens nearby.

One of the boys was smiling from ear to ear. He beamed with pride as he said it again, "Hey! What up my nigga!" It was so unnatural for his tongue, so unfitting for his mouth. Before I could respond, a sense of guilt and shame fell over me. In a serious tone I shook his hand and said "Ain't no niggas here. Brother. Call me brother."

They all looked at me with disappointment. Here they were trying to relate to me, the Black

American. The N-word was supposed to be a rite of passage and I denied them of an exchange I have all the time. I thwarted their attempt to live out some American pop culture fantasy. *Why do Americans get to have all the fun? Why couldn't we be niggas together?*

That night I reevaluated my use of the word, but the interaction also made me question my identity. I considered the split between Africans and Black Americans, between the citizens of the continent and those of us taken from it. Some Americans feel a sense of longing and deep connection, and there are some who feel that couldn't be farther from the truth.

Our sense of nationalism is divided. We are kin by color, but the deeper connection needed for community is culture; this is where we get lost in the diaspora. The space between African and American grows more wide over time, while our politically correct titles become faux attempts of reconciliation.

The N-word has lived a thousand lives. The NAACP even tried to bury it, yet it rose again on the third day. It's always been a chameleon, blending its way into American culture one shade at a time. The word was not ours. It was created by the racist, and somehow we took ownership and reinterpreted its definition. We made a new nigga, but control, or power for Blacks in a white world has always been relative.

I am one of the biggest fans of our ability to influence and stylize language, but control yields to power. We use all of our imagination to bend and flex the nigga, but industry has bought the rights to distribution. Men in suits take our words from our mama's basement for gain just for men in suits to, in turn, use our words against us. They condemn the very language they use for profit. We have to sit in the middle of all these biased agendas that could care less about Black Culture and the historical context of the language and word in question. Before we could even get a grip on the N-word, before we could even get a grip on our identity, our voices, a fraction of our likeness was being copied, manufactured, and sold around the world.

I'm torn. We're torn—the dichotomy of the N-word's use is obvious in every generation from our elders to our youth. Here we are conflicted about our common view of acceptance or opposition, and now everyone wants to get in on the conversation. The nigga's identity within mainstream channels is seen as permission for everyone to be the N-word. As I would learn on that day in Accra even the original niggers want to be niggas.

The power of words, the bridges they build, the wounds they heal, the futures they paint, whether spoken or written, words connect us through time and space. However, I would be a fool to ignore the tragedies of the tongue: the walls it builds, the scars it leaves, the history it erases. The N-word is no different. Without the power to teach and control context we can only make something bitter, palatable. But all sugar ain't sweet.

A BLUES FOR NINA& BARBARA& MAYA&

```
& I'm just      a man
                        at times
Just            a dog
                        at times
Just            frustrated
                A fist
                        at times
                A traitor
                        at times
I just          Cain
                        at times
For your body is always
                able.
```

```
                    They try so hard to break you
                    Because they heard

                            Black don't      crack
                    They just want to see you   crack
                    Want to hear you         crack
                    Want to touch your       cracks
                    Want to feel your        cracks
                    Want to commoditize your cracks
                    Want to divide us into   cracks
                    Want to point out these  cracks

                    Just so they can say
                    She's not all she's      cracked
                                             up to be.
```

```
            I may never live long enough
            to understand your divinity,
            How you endure you walking earthquake,
            You even disaster beautifully

            The Black & the Woman
            Never without plight.
```

You're proud of yourself. Hell, you should be. You made it. You achieved that dream. You passed another milestone. All your hard work paid off. Every sacrifice was worth it. But you can't sacrifice everything, and you are reminded of that fact. You dot every 'i' and cross every 't' nicely, careful not to brush outside the lines. Still, there's something a little off.

You will hear everything under the sun. You're told you don't smile enough. You're told about your attitude, about your confidence, about how you speak, how you dress, how you style your hair, even how you laugh. The common thread here is how inadequacy is forced upon you through a biased lens. A lens that wants to see itself in everything. Naturally it cannot see itself in you, so it attempts to control what it cannot change. You don't fit the picture.

By tradition, it is your natural being—the tone of your skin and texture of your hair—that has been offensive to all things American. All things white. It's best for the sake of approval you show as less of your Black as possible. If you really want to stay the course, you must deny yourself of yourself—shrink that "Blackness" into a question, making sure to not assert, but ask for permission. Silence is your golden ticket to integration.

In order to obtain superficial status or monetary worth, you end up relinquishing your culture. You begin to tolerate and ignore the bigotry in the room. You don't want to ruffle feathers because you have encroached enough already. If you just continue to do well, they will see that you belong. You can earn a place. You can earn their trust by keeping up the good work. You can gain equality by your merits. They will see you as more than just Black.

Until, of course, you are exposed before the world and forced to show your true color. The moment in time when you can no longer take the injustices; the one time you can't dodge the bullet, and you speak up about it. You raise your voice, not even to contest, but to express concern. It can be as sincere as a call for help, however, that call for help is the moment you choose yourself and not them.

They will not bow to hear you out. They will be taken aback, floored in disbelief that you could take a stand, or stand with your arms at your side, or sit, or sit straight, or kneel, or pray, or do anything opposite of what they're doing. They thought you were one of them. They thought you were above it all. They expected more from you, because you exceeded their expectations. Yes, you're Black, but there's something different about you. You speak so well. You work so hard. You're such a good person at heart. What happened to you?

For once a good nigger always a good nigger, and it isn't wise to disappoint.

It was business as usual. The train was packed during the morning commute, even the typical train delay was right on schedule. Everyone was normal, everything was routine and that was the problem. This was not just another day. First Alton Sterling then Philando Castile—I should've been able to call in sick. I was battling the symptoms from a vicious disease called racism that killed two more innocent Black men.

I needed time to heal but I didn't get that time. I went to work like most of us, not sure of what to expect of my colleagues or myself. I arrived a shell of who I normally am, but I still showed up. For four days I showed up for work, but the humanity of my colleagues never made it in. There was a war going on outside, and they hadn't noticed, as if the war didn't include them. I was the lone soldier praying to God I make it back home in one piece.

I imagined them racking their brains on how to initiate conversation about excessive police force and prejudice in the line of duty. When the topics never came up, I still gave them the benefit of the doubt. I thought maybe they hadn't heard yet, but of course they did. They chose to disengage, and once again I felt the sharp force of silence and indifference.

It was the same feeling I had the day Prince died. I was working out of a coffee shop in Ft. Greene—white-owned of course, and I was the shot of diversity—I was trying to work out some new material, but of course I was all in my feelings. I looked around, and everyone else was good. To my surprise, Prince began to play over the room. For a few minutes I felt appreciated, I felt like I mattered, and then just like that the tribute was over. It was a gesture, an act of acknowledgement, but not of necessity. They didn't play Prince because they needed to hear his voice, but rather it was a nice thing to do.

I remember thinking I wish I knew of a Black-owned coffee spot where I could be among my people. I just wanted to be in the midst, in an environment where I could meet eyes with someone and we'd both just get it. I wanted to be understood, embraced, and cared for. I wanted to know others cared about my world. Too often my reality is predicated on fitting into another world, joining a conversation already in full swing, attempting to carve out space for myself and my culture.

Black America and white America are two distinct worlds sharing the same land. The scales of power however always lean in favor of the latter. If America is to reach its ideals and live out its theoretical creeds, the conversation must be had with everyone at the table. The interests must be equal and balanced. The roles of power must exchange hands often. Otherwise, we'll continue to feel like we're on the outside looking in, even in the face of our own stories.

It bothers me that it's so difficult to have a healthy conversation, that I can't be taken serious because I come off to white America as if I'm attacking their names and their nation. (White America is any person, place or thing that embraces and esteems this country on the foundation of race, perpetuates discriminatory practices, and turns a blind eye to inequality.) The aloof response from white circles is a clear sign of the fundamental differences dividing our country. This great nation has a million suggestions on what Black people should do, but it does not show up for us. It only shows up for itself, it only shows up to be the hero.

The goal of any society is to establish a status quo, enforce order, and uphold the power structure. Diversity is more about presence than power. We arrive into these diverse spaces only to be rewarded with indifference and censorship. Everyone is suppressed by the pursuit of the American Dream. We are induced to be neutral and patient for change. The energy required to "get in where you fit in" has its long term effects, and the older we get the more compliant we become.

I am tasked to master the ability to shift and bend to ensure the comfort of others. But who will protect the blind spot in the middle of my consciousness? Who will stand up and speak out for Black America in my place when I am weak? We cannot be the only group that realizes the pride of the oppressed is feeble in the hands of its oppressors. White flight has to stop. The only influence we have on white behavior cannot be to flee both physically and emotionally. Our neighbors and colleagues need to stop to consider the war going on, and step up and be allies. If not, then we can only assume they have chosen the side of the oppressor. The reality of "Blackness" around the world will never change if we continue accommodating white sensitivity and the white imagination. Enough with the silence already; somebody say something!

THESE NAMES THEY HAVE

You know these names they have,
they say make too much noise.
They say the names be spelled funny.
Be too many syllables,

A	punch line.
A	red flag.
A	security risk.
A	bull's eye.
A	target.

Just like the president,
and he has one of those names too.
Mama named him Ba-rack.
And who they saying Mrs. Obama's baby
boy be?

Osama bin,
Hussein,

All sound the same.
Sound like sadam,
Like islam,
Like the type of name you drop,

Sounds like a bomb.

But what about the war on him,
the terror on them with a name that
sounds like Derrion,

Danroy,
Trayvon,
Rekia,
Ezell,
Ramarley,

Sounds like I've heard this before.
Funny how the names sound the same,
but aint nobody laughing
but the grave.
Got his mouth wide open
And can't hold all these
Black bodies in.

Tamir,
Renisha,
Laquan,
Alton,
Delrawn,
Philando,
Deravis,
Korryn,
Kouren,

Security at Radio City Music Hall called me out. It was a Gotye concert, and my acquaintances and I looked like the board of trustees for diversity: white guy, Asian girl, ambiguous Black girl, and me. It was a last-second invite and I said *sure why not? What's the worst that can happen?*

We were seconds from the lobby, after passing through what I thought was the security checkpoint, when I heard the charming words, "Excuse me sir, can you empty your pockets?" (Which to me sounded like, "Step out of the car!" or "Let me see your hands!") My mind went blank. I couldn't decipher if I was feeling shock or embarrassment. Double consciousness took over, and the out of body experience ensued. All I was worried about was how everyone else perceived me in the moment.

Shock crept in quickly. I couldn't believe someone of my character could be questioned. Embarrassment soon followed, and I'm seeing what everyone else sees, another Black body on display for judgment. I thought I escaped misunderstandings such as this. I thought I was above it.

It's a matter of seconds before I realize that I've been putting on all day, maybe all month, hell, maybe even all my life. I wonder who have I been all this time. Here I am, wearing my best face for company and it's still not enough. Some random guy, with a random job title, still has enough authority to remind everyone that I'm just another nigga.

He stopped me dead in my tracks and didn't think twice about it. I had a right to be upset. I had a right to check him, but I couldn't get out of my head. I went through the motions of compliance. I did what I was accustomed to doing; I exercised my meek and humble right to remain silent and do as I'm told.

I played it safe and respectable, because I know what happens when we reach for privilege the world has never given us. I told myself, not to worry, it would all be over soon enough, but it's never over. I couldn't stop thinking about it. I couldn't enjoy myself that night. I tried to have a good time, but my mind was stuck in that moment. It's cruel, the way victims are always left with the burden of trying to make sense of another's wretched crime.

A random Gotye concert became just another memory to add to the file of doing normal and harmless things while Black. I think about what would've happened had I lost my cool. I should've snapped, but the repercussions of utilizing my freedom of speech is always hanging over my head. I know that in this society I am guilty until proven innocent.

On a separate occasion, I remember when a buddy of mine felt the gravity of white privilege, and he didn't choose the high ground. A group of us were leaving a lounge in Chinatown, and I had just hailed a cab. As I was getting in, a white girl jumped in from the other side. I leaned into the car to tell her she can exit now, when all of a sudden my friend rushed to the other side to pull her out of the car.

My first thought—*Black man. White woman. Liqour. Problem.* I ran around the cab and grabbed him before the night went left. The disrespect took him over the top. He lost it. He snapped, but I knew his frustration. I'll never forget the pain in his eyes when he said, "I'm sick of this Cyrus! They always do this shit! They always get away with this."

He wasn't talking about a cab anymore. He was talking about the daily reminders that confirm our biggest fear. The fear that we live outside of the protection of human rights. Our safety, our existence is not guaranteed. We are susceptible to the flaws of a social construct, and we must render ourselves defenseless. Our life comes with consequence with or without our input, and somehow they will find a way to blame us. Black life is probable cause and here we are, target practice to conventional racism. They want us to follow orders while they shoot first, and ask questions later.

WHO

IN MEMORY OF AMIRI

WHO	said you posed a threat	?
WHO	said you fit the description	?
WHO	said all yall look alike	?
WHO	forgot what a gun looks like	?
WHO	didn't give you time to reach for your	
	license and registration	?
WHO	confused your wallet or cellphone for a weapon	?
WHO	only needs a technicality to shoot	?
WHO	didn't care that you were scared	?
WHO	didn't care that you were a child	?
WHO	didn't care that your mother told you to get home safe	?
WHO	didn't care that you were a father of five	?
WHO	didn't care that your daughter was in the back seat	?
WHO	pulled their gun on you	?
WHO	forgot you human	?
WHO	shot you	?
WHO	was just doing their job, when they shot you	?
WHOSE	job is to shoot	?
WHO	shoots to kill	?
WHOSE	shots rang out	?
WHO	valued the life of a bullet over yours	?
WHO	went home to his wife and child	
	when you didn't make it down the block	?
WHO	gon' clean this one up	?
WHO	gon' tell his momma	?
WHO	gon' show up to momma's front door with cameras	
	and questions instead of compassion and care	?
WHO	care more about the feature than her feelings	?
WHO	gon' try and settle momma with settlement money	?
WHO	even cares	?
WHO	heard this before	?
WHO	heard this time and time again	?
WHO	sick and tired	?
WHO	sick and tired of being sick and tired	?
WHO	gon' do something about it	?

WHO will we bury next ?

Sam Dubose was shot in the head at point blank range. The man who killed him was police officer Ray Tensing. It was a routine traffic stop that went wrong (by wrong I mean Officer Tensing's decision to pull his gun out was premature, careless, arrogant, and fatal.) Sam was dead; car slammed into a tree, and there was Tensing running behind the car with his gun out.

Another Black life gone, and the first people who could pay respect and acknowledge the loss of life, barely paid Sam any attention. It was as if he was supposed to die. The irony of a dead Black man being overshadowed by the implications of why he's dead in the first place is strange, bizarre, and authentically American. The other responding officers seemed more concerned with what was to come for their fellow man in blue and not the man sitting in his own blood.

In the body cam footage, Officer Tensing doesn't come off tense or stressed. He is indifferent—watching this video makes me sick to my stomach. It's obvious that he chooses to protect himself and his fellow officers act accordingly. He evades responsibility of this moral infraction and turns his back to the magnitude of the situation. When asked if he is okay, he responds about his arm being hurt. He just killed a man for no reason at all, and his arm hurts.

Well my heart hurts. Not only did I have to sit through an execution in broad daylight, in a neighborhood that looks all too familiar, but I also had to watch another police officer dismiss another Black life.

I hate the way we have to watch Black bodies endure various forms of brutality, however, if we didn't have proof, who would believe us? This recurring imagery has to have a perversive effect on our compassion. If people can be outraged about the shooting of a zoo animal, but somehow be torn about a human, then maybe we've already reached the tipping point.

We are still fighting for equality. Black lives matter in spaces of entertainment, but we are not given a place to share our voices elsewhere. Will the deaths of innocent Black bodies ever be despicable to everyone? Will Americans ever take the murders of Sam, Trayvon, Jordan, Tyre or Renisha personally? Will the nation cry over these deaths? Or has American history robbed its citizens of the ability to feel intimate compassion for non-white life?

DAMN JOE

I wonder if it will ever hit home
the way bullets do in Chicago.

        Where living rooms are living
wounds that never heal
        Where lemonade stands stand
like barricades
        Buses ride like armored trucks
        through roadside bombs
        dressed as high school
        students
        We hold the flags of warring
nations
        The windy got a wayward way
        blowing Black boys back behind
enemy lines
        Where hurricane fingers flip
gang signs
        that shake up communities
faster than news flashes
••
NEWS FLASH:
you don't need a meteorologist
to tell you fatherless homes
blossom in inclement weather
where politicians are fair weather
calling the city a warzone
with no intent on making it better

Segregation forced us to build our own and do for self. Among many other things, white supremacy refused us freedom, mobility and advancement. In spite of it all, we built our own stores, our own banks, our own hospitals and universities. We chose to ensure our own quality of life, instead of wasting away under the hand of oppression. The same hand— holding the whip, holding the torch, holding the dogs, holding the guns, holding us captive— took our self-sufficiency and destroyed it. This is the history that sets the stage for the troubles of today's Black elite. Today's Black athlete.

Those of us with the biggest spotlight say the least in fear of losing everything. We have taken over the sports arena in numbers, but somehow that doesn't equate to power. The billion dollar business is built on our backs and we choose to mind our own. Even the highly paid superstars act as if they too, can be destroyed. Their brands are bigger than life, but when problems arise that are close to home, they are nowhere to be found. It's conflicting to admire the notoriety that comes along with professional sports, when many stars avoid shedding light on societal issues to maintain the luster of their brands.

However, in a superficial society, much of the admiration of Black athletes is fairweather, at best. Fans laud them, dressing them in superlatives and powerful nicknames, yet assassinate their character when they step out of bounds. If a Black athlete celebrates too freely, he is critiqued for lacking sportsmanship. If a bare-chested fan screams, yells, boos or boogies in front of a dance cam, it's all just a part of the experience. These double standards are blatant, and will remain if our Black athletes don't challenge the systems in place.

I see a plantation that wants its Black bodies physically sharp without intellectual poise. Accountability and leadership are virtues to be exhausted on (or maybe, in) the field. I hear the crack of the whip every time a reporter suggests a Black athlete is lucky to have the chance to play a sport; as if to say a group of white men granted him his God-given abilities. The Black athlete is expected and instructed to shut up and do his job. He receives pressure from the millionaire owner who tells him to consider the fans who paid their hard-earned money, and from the coach who calls anything outside the game a "distraction."

Over time the desire to speak openly about anything outside the lines of sports becomes dormant under the foot of compliance and progress. The Black athlete is told he must play by the rules if he wants in. I sympathize for those who sacrifice integrity for integration. They are so frightened of falling from grace, that they refuse to stand for anything. The Black athlete emerges from his circumstance with every intention to give back. He's a role model and an inspiration to the community. But his hands are tied. Individual success has filled his pockets, while draining his self sufficiency. He thinks being the face is enough, but what is a face without a voice?

If our Black athletes only receive support when they do things "the right way" (the white way) by adhering to their system, then something is wrong. Sure, the community drives and charity events are helpful, but we have to ask if "the powers that be" truly care? Does the league get behind its athletes for the people or the press? Are these teams committed to their image, or the rights of their players?

The legacy of the late Muhammad Ali is less about sport and more about his character. Ali will forever be respected for not submitting to a culture of intimidation and fear. Throughout his career he stood on his beliefs. He stood in front of the camera with millions of people watching, and told the world the truth, not some politically correct pageant speech. He didn't dance around topics or talk in circles. Ali never dismissed the injustices endemic to white supremacy or put the blame on us. He sacrificed his career for the sake of his life, our lives, and that's an act of greatness.

Talent may earn accolades, but the man or woman you are is what earns respect. Take a knee!

OUTRO

If you're a smart Negro
Who chooses to run
You need to know they will not look for you
They will only look for your body
That human spirit you possess is insignificant
You best hide
And hide good

If you're a smart Negro
You know the one thing that matters more than what can be chased
Is what can be caught
They catch you better than they keep you
They love like punishment
Affirm like slur
Kiss like shackle
Cuddle like noose

If you're a smart Negro
You know the world is your abuser
They taught you to take a punch and smile
Taught you to take a beating and hang on
You know how to be strong
You just don't know how to use your strength
And they only get stronger

If you're a smart Negro
You know power is relative
The nigger is a necessity
If you're not in the picture
Whose life will they steal
Whose knowledge will they pillage
Whose contributions will they call their own

But a smart Negro
Has a mouth of his own
Can speak well
But even a smart Negro is unaware of his native tongue
That's why they refuse to hear you
They only hear themselves
They hear the white soap used to wash your African mouth clean
All that English forced down your throat

If you're a smart Negro you sound treacherous
You sound like things are changing
Sound like additional mouths to feed
Too many seats at the table
This is why they don't see you
They're busy watching you
Too busy keeping an eye on you

If you're a smart Negro you know
A jar with a lid on it is practical
A jar with no lid can be messy
Always ready to escape containment
You're always looking for a way out
You're always looking for a way home

If you're a smart Negro
You know it's easier to run alone
But you ain't never been that smart

~ ~ ~

AFTERTHOUGHT

I'm exhausted. I'm working as fast as I can. I can't think fast enough. I can't write fast enough. We don't last long enough. They keep it up. I can't keep up. It's not enough. It's never enough. One wasn't enough. Emmett Till. Wasn't enough. Four little girls. Wasn't enough. Central Park Five. Wasn't enough. Jena Six. Wasn't enough. Charleston Nine. Wasn't enough. My Father wasn't enough. Her son wasn't enough. His daughter ain't enough. Their Mother ain't enough. God ain't enough. These prayers ain't strong enough. Barack wasn't enough. Change ain't enough. Ain't come soon enough. They gon' kill us all. Then what. Then what. More protests. More riots. More violence. More sirens. I can't hear myself. Can't hear no help. Here by myself. To die alone. No one else. Knows this hell. They know damn well. The hell. I Can't stand. Can't stand. Can't kneel. Can't sit. Can't speak. I Can't. But they can. I Can't. But they can. As they please. As they see fit. Makes no sense. They so quiet. One sided. Shots fired. I won't quiet. I won't quit. Don't quit. Don't quit.

Cyrus Aaron © 2016

Designed by Helen Koh
Edited by Ditte Woodson

st Edition
978-0998178004

oursinfo@gmail.com
hrs.com